Nine Days To

STRENGTHEN YOUR FAITH

Nine Days To

STRENGTHEN YOUR FAITH

JACQUES PHILIPPE

Scepter

Nine days to…

Collection edited by Timothée Berthon

The "Nine Days to" collection offers a guided retreat to be lived at home or on vacation, in the subway or on the train, for people who have little time but wish to devote ten minutes a day to spiritual growth.

Each book in the collection offers nine days of inspiring meditations that surround a specific theme for advancement in the spiritual life. Each serves as both a school of prayer and an authentic tool of self-transformation.

Two meditations are offered for each day. One can be experienced in the morning and the other at any opportune moment during the day or evening.

The journey includes reflection exercises, the Word of God, a meditation from a saint or another great spiritual author, and a resolution—all geared to help the participant dive into an authentic spiritual experience.

JACQUES PHILIPPE

Published by Scepter Publishers, Inc.
info@scepterpublishers.org
www.scepterpublishers.org
800-322-8773
New York

Text and cover design: Rose Design
Cover image: Majid Rangraz on Unsplash.com

Library of Congress Control Number: 2020941399

PB ISBN: 9781594173974
eBook ISBN: 9781594173981

Printed in the United States of America

Contents

First Day

FAITH, A SOURCE OF LIFE

Daily Mediation

INVITATION TO CONTEMPLATION

I take a few moments to compose myself. I put myself in the present moment. . . . I breathe calmly. I put aside all worries and stress, and I confidently welcome God's presence. He is here, close to me, and he loves me.

SIGN OF THE CROSS

In the name of the Father, and of the Son, and of the Holy Spirit. Amen.

PRAYER TO THE HOLY SPIRIT

Holy Spirit, you who are light, you who are the consoler, come and guide my prayer today. Come fill me with your soft presence; awaken my heart to God's love. Make trust and faith grow in me.

MEDITATION FROM
FR. JACQUES PHILIPPE

During this retreat, we are going to meditate on faith and ask God to grow our faith. This is the most important thing for each one of us.

Faith is a reality that's a little paradoxical. On the one hand, it's a simple thing, a disposition of the heart, often lived through poverty and dryness. But on the other hand, it's a very beautiful, fruitful reality, because faith, the act of faith, truly puts us in contact with God and opens us little by little to all the richness and depth of the mystery of God. Any progress in faith brings progress in hope and in love. Faith is the only light that never deceives us. It is, in fact, our true strength. It allows us to lean on God.

We could say that, in a sense, all our sins and all our faults come from a lack of faith. We don't believe enough in God's power and love, and in the end that is our real problem.

It's true that we sometimes live through difficult and painful circumstances, which can be tough to confront. We also often experience our own weakness and frailty. Nevertheless, these difficulties are not our real problem. Our only problem is our lack of faith. If we live through our difficulties and personal limits with faith, if we put them in God's hands with full trust, he will take care of us, and even those events in our lives that seem to be the most negative will wind up being positive.

In the Gospels, Jesus insists on the importance of faith:

> If you had faith the size of a mustard seed, you would say to this mountain, "Move from here to there," and it would move (cf. Mt 17:20; similar in Lk 17:6). What Jesus most reproaches the disciples for is not their human weakness, but their lack of faith.

When we read the Gospel of John, we find a whole list of the benefits that come from faith: He who believes is not judged but passes from death to life, walks in light, has eternal life, is never thirsty; even if he dies he will live, will see the glory of God, is already resurrected, will do works like Christ did and even still greater ones, and is victorious over the world (cf. 1 Jn 5:4).

At the end of his gospel, John says, "Now Jesus did many other signs in the presence of his disciples, which are not written in this book. But these are written so that you may come to believe that Jesus is the Messiah, the Son of God, and that through believing you may have life in his name" (Jn 20:30–31).

You will have life in his name!

This is essential: Faith gives us life, real life on this earth, the eternal life of the Kingdom. It puts us in true contact with God, lets us touch God. And our God is the God of life!

PRAYER

Let us entrust ourselves to the Virgin Mary, guardian of our faith.

Hail Mary, full of grace, the Lord is with thee. Blessed art thou among women and blessed is the fruit of thy womb, Jesus. Holy Mary, Mother of God, pray for us, sinners, now and at the hour of our death. Amen.

A Grace to Request

I reflect on all the times I've lacked faith, and how that is my principal problem. I ask Jesus to make me grow in faith.

Light from a Faithful Witness

"He who has faith penetrates into God and rivers of life flow from his being: this is spiritual fruitfulness."

—Bl. Marie-Eugène of the Child Jesus, OCD

Meditate on the Word

In chapter 11 of John's Gospel, before resurrecting Lazarus, Jesus speaks to Martha:

> Jesus said to her, "I am the resurrection and the life. Those who believe in me, even though they die, will live, and everyone who lives and believes in me will never die. Do you believe this?" She said to him, "Yes, Lord, I believe that you are the Messiah, the Son of God, the one coming into the world." (Jn 11:25–27)

I memorize these words and repeat them to myself often during the day:

"Everyone who lives and believes in me will never die."

BLESSING

May the almighty and merciful God bless us and keep us. The Father, the Son, and the Holy Spirit. Amen.

Second Day

My Faith Is the Faith of the Church

Daily Meditation

INVITATION TO CONTEMPLATION

I take a few moments to compose myself. I put myself in the present moment. . . . I breathe calmly. I put aside all worries and stress, and I confidently welcome God's presence. He is here, close to me, and he loves me.

SIGN OF THE CROSS

In the name of the Father, and of the Son, and of the Holy Spirit. Amen.

PRAYER TO THE HOLY SPIRIT

Holy Spirit, you who are light, you who are the consoler, come and guide my prayer today. Come fill me with your soft presence; awaken my heart to God's love. Make trust and faith grow in me.

MEDITATION FROM
FR. JACQUES PHILIPPE

There is a very personal, intimate dimension to an act of faith. No one can believe on my behalf.

And in this personal act of faith, there are two inseparable aspects: obedience and trust.

It's an act of obedience because to believe is to accept a truth that surpasses me: I am not the master. It means submitting my intelligence to the light of God, letting myself be led by him. It means making him the Lord of my life. In the letter to the Hebrews, it is said about Abraham, "By faith Abraham obeyed when he was called to set out for a place that he was to receive as an inheritance; and he set out, not knowing where he was going" (Heb 11:8).

Faith is a beautiful adventure; we don't always know where it will lead us!

But this act of faith is also an act of trust. We know that God loves us and that he wants our happiness. To believe is to trust, to place ourselves in the hands of God like little children who surrender themselves into their father's arms.

We also must note that even if faith is a very personal belonging to God, it has within its content the objective side of faith—an important community dimension. My faith is the faith of the Church. Today, we have the tendency to make up our own personal beliefs according to our taste and the times; we take a little of this and a little of that as it pleases us in order to make up our own little religion.

But this isn't the Christian faith. My faith isn't an individualistic reality that I've made up; it's something that I receive. My faith is the faith of Mary, the faith of the Apostles; it's the faith that the Church transmits from generation to generation, and it's one that I can't cover with my own little sauce, or it loses its force and its beauty. Of course, this faith can be expressed differently during different times and by different cultures, but it is one faith in its essentials.

Remember the words of St. Paul in the Letter to the Ephesians: "Just as you were called to the one hope of your calling, one Lord, one faith, one baptism, one God and Father of all, who is above all and through all and in all" (Eph 4:4–6).

Growing in faith, getting to the fullness of faith "little by little," according to the expression in the letter to the Hebrews, is then a double movement: one part an act of belonging to God that's more and more personal, free, deep, and living; and one part better understanding the content and richness of our faith. May our intellect always be more and more open with joy to all the "mysteries" of the Gospel and the Christian faith.

The two aspects of faith, the subjective aspect—this personal act of belonging—and the objective aspect—the content of faith, the truths to which we adhere—are actually closely linked to each other. Pope Emeritus Benedict XVI said, "There exists a profound unity between the act by which we believe and the content to which we give our assent."[1]

The more sincere and profound the personal act of belonging, of trust and obedience, the more the richness of the content of faith is

1. Benedict XVI, Apostolic Letter *Porta Fidei* (Rome: Libreria Editrice Vaticana, October 11, 2011), par. 10.

revealed and becomes accessible. And the converse is also true, as the more the content of faith is discovered in its truth, its richness, and its beauty, the more the act of belonging, of putting oneself in the hands of God, will be strong and free, and will truly realize its fruitfulness.

Faith is an adventure, as we don't know where it will lead us; at the same time, it offers us great security, for it puts us in the arms of God and gathers us in the light that doesn't mislead, the certitude of the truths that God brings forth in our lives.

PRAYER

Let us entrust ourselves to the Virgin Mary, guardian of our faith.

> Hail Mary, full of grace, the Lord is with thee. Blessed art thou among women and blessed is the fruit of thy womb, Jesus. Holy Mary, Mother of God, pray for us, sinners, now and at the hour of our death. Amen.

A Grace to Request

Better understanding the faith is not simply a personal option. Rather, believing means sharing the faith of the whole Church. I ask God for a greater desire to deepen my knowledge of the truths in which I believe, and that my belonging to him may happen with ever greater trust.

Light from a Faithful Witness

"Faith is not an isolated act. No one can believe alone, just as no one can live alone. You have not given yourself faith as you have not given yourself life."

—*Catechism of the Catholic Church*, par. 166

Meditate on the Word

In the Letter to the Ephesians, Paul says the following:

> I therefore, the prisoner in the Lord, beg you to lead a life worthy of the calling to which you have been called, with all humility and gentleness, with patience, bearing with one

another in love, making every effort to maintain the unity of the Spirit in the bond of peace. There is one body and one Spirit, just as you were called to the one hope of your calling, one Lord, one faith, one baptism, one God and Father of all. (Eph 4:1–6)

I keep this in my heart and repeat these words during my day:

"There is one Lord, one faith, one baptism, one God and Father of all."

BLESSING

May the almighty and merciful God bless us and keep us. The Father, the Son, and the Holy Spirit. Amen.

Third Day

FAITH: GIFT OF GOD AND HUMAN DECISION

Daily Meditation

INVITATION TO CONTEMPLATION

I take a few moments to compose myself. I put myself in the present moment. . . . I breathe calmly. I put aside all worries and stress, and I confidently welcome God's presence. He is here, close to me, and he loves me.

SIGN OF THE CROSS

In the name of the Father, and of the Son, and of the Holy Spirit. Amen.

PRAYER TO THE HOLY SPIRIT

Holy Spirit, you who are light, you who are the consoler, come and guide my prayer today. Come fill me with your soft presence; awaken my heart to God's love. Make trust and faith grow in me.

MEDITATION FROM
FR. JACQUES PHILIPPE

Today we are going to meditate on other important aspects of faith. It is partly a gift from God, a grace, but also partly a personal decision.

Faith is a gift from God: This is clearly expressed in the Scriptures. Jesus says, "No one can come to me unless drawn by the Father who sent me" (Jn 6:44).

And it's because the Holy Spirit lights our hearts that we can believe.

Faith is a gift of God's mercy. It isn't based upon personal merit; it's simply a gift that he gives us, whether through our education, from our family, or by the grace of a moment of conversion.

The true believer is never someone who judges or disdains others because they don't believe. The believer knows that faith was given freely.

The believer thanks the Lord for faith, but doesn't allow a conceited self-estimation. Pope Francis says, "One who believes may not be presumptuous; on the contrary, truth leads to humility, since believers know that, rather than ourselves possessing truth, it is truth that embraces and possesses us.[1]

But this gift from God comes through a personal decision: Faith is also a decision by a person, a fully human act. It is an act that is possible thanks to God's help, but an act that also implicates our freedom, our intelligence, and our will.

There are moments in life when faith is natural, easy. But there are other moments when it is a courageous decision, a fight. We could have a thousand reasons to doubt, to not trust God, to revolt against him, but, in spite of all that, we decide to believe.

This fight is what St. Thérèse of Lisieux lived through at the end of her life. She entered into a very sorrowful period, full of suffering and trials, not only because of her sickness, but also because of strong temptations against faith and hope. She used to say things like, "I have made more acts of faith in this last year than during

1. Francis, Encyclical Letter *Lumen Fidei* (Rome: Libreria Editrice Vaticana, June 29, 2013), par. 34.

all the rest of my life," and "I believe what I want to believe!"

She always carried with her the Creed written in her own blood, to show her determination to believe, in spite of the suffering and the doubts that tormented her. Her faithfulness in believing is certainly a gift from God, but she had to put all her courage and determination into it, as well.

We all have analogous moments when faith can no longer be a convenience, a habit of thinking, but when it must become a courageous decision. These moments are not pleasant to live through, but it is during these moments that faith really becomes a personal choice, that it gets deeper, and that it matures into an adult faith.

Another one of faith's paradoxes is that it is both light and darkness. It is a great light, the most precious of all light, because it gives us access to the truth about God, about the profound sense to our life and how to orient it. Faith lights our way and enlightens our decisions.

But it is also darkness: Many of faith's truths surpass our intelligence, our capacity to understand. St. Paul says, "O the depth of the riches and wisdom and knowledge of God! How unsearchable are his judgments and how inscrutable his ways!" (Rom 11:33).

Faith is not contrary to intelligence, but surpasses it. It makes us accept truths larger than intelligence can grasp.

Living in faith means walking in light, but doesn't mean that we can understand everything, explain everything, master everything— far from it. Sometimes we see what we believe, but sometimes we must believe without seeing, to accept plodding along in a bit of darkness while putting all our trust in God.

PRAYER

Let us entrust ourselves to the Virgin Mary, guardian of our faith.

> Hail Mary, full of grace, the Lord is with thee.
> Blessed art thou among women and blessed

is the fruit of thy womb, Jesus. Holy Mary, Mother of God, pray for us, sinners, now and at the hour of our death. Amen.

A Grace to Request

I thank God for the gift of faith that he gave me, the greatest gift that he could give me. I also ask him that this decision for faith be ever stronger in me, in moments of joy as well as difficult moments, in moments of light and of darkness. May I always remain determined to believe.

Light from a Faithful Witness

"To make this act of faith, the grace of God and the interior help of the Holy Spirit must precede and assist, moving the heart and turning it to God, opening the eyes of the mind and giving 'joy and ease to everyone in assenting to the truth and believing it.'"

—Pope St. Paul VI, Dogmatic Constitution on Divine Revelation *Dei verbum*, par. 5

MEDITATE ON THE WORD

In the Gospel of Matthew, the disciples are in a boat crossing the lake, battered by the wind and the waves. Jesus joins them by walking on the water. They are frightened and take him for a ghost. Jesus says, "'Take heart, it is I; do not be afraid.' Peter answered him, 'Lord, if it is you, command me to come to you on the water.' He said, 'Come.' So Peter got out of the boat, started walking on the water, and came toward Jesus. But when he noticed the strong wind, he became frightened, and beginning to sink, he cried out, 'Lord, save me!' Jesus immediately reached out his hand and caught him, saying to him, 'You of little faith, why did you doubt?'" (Mt 14:27–31).

I keep this in my heart and repeat often this sentence:

"Take heart, it is I; do not be afraid!"

BLESSING

May the almighty and merciful God bless us and keep us. The Father, the Son, and the Holy Spirit. Amen.

Fourth Day

FAITH, HOPE, AND LOVE

Daily Meditation

INVITATION TO CONTEMPLATION

I take a few moments to compose myself. I put myself in the present moment. . . . I breathe calmly. I put aside all worries and stress, and I confidently welcome God's presence. He is here, close to me, and he loves me.

SIGN OF THE CROSS

In the name of the Father, and of the Son, and of the Holy Spirit. Amen.

PRAYER TO THE HOLY SPIRIT

Holy Spirit, you who are light, you who are the consoler, come and guide my prayer today. Come fill me with your soft presence; awaken my heart to God's love. Make trust and faith grow in me.

MEDITATION FROM
FR. JACQUES PHILIPPE

Today we are going to meditate on the beautiful link between faith, hope, and love.

We cannot disassociate faith from these other two theological virtues: hope and charity. These virtues are called the theological virtues because they unite us to God, letting us enter into God's life. They are a gift from God but also a decision by man. They are truly the heart of Christian life, as St. Paul highlights in his letters.

Charity—love—is the ultimate goal, whereas faith and hope will pass away. When we are in heaven, we won't need faith anymore, because we will see God, and we won't need hope anymore, because we will already possess everything for which we hoped. Only love will remain.

But in our journey on the earth, love cannot do without faith and hope, since it relies on them. Faith engenders hope, and faith and hope give us the strength to love. Faith and hope are like the two wings that let love take flight, carrying it ever higher.

But if faith and hope diminish, love will grow cold. A lack of fervor, of generosity, often comes from discouragement, from a loss of hope and of faith. We don't believe anymore, so we lower our arms.

When we are fearful, doubtful, worried, or discouraged, the heart closes and becomes incapable of loving.

We must also recognize that loving isn't always easy, and that some acts of love, like forgiveness or love of enemies, require a lot of hope and faith.

But we can also say that, in another sense, faith itself is the product of love: The deepest expression of love is openness to another and trust. The more love grows, the stronger trust becomes. True faith is already in itself an act of love: It makes us accept God in his divine truth and permits us to give ourselves to him, return to him with trust and obedience.

The faith described in the Gospel is inseparable from love. Without works of love, it is a "dead faith" like James says (Jas 2:14–18).

We speak of a "faith immersed in love," saturated by love. St. John of the Cross speaks of "the faith with which we love God without understanding him."[1]

Pope Emeritus Benedict XVI says, "Faith without charity bears no fruit, while charity without faith would be a sentiment constantly at the mercy of doubt. Faith and charity each require the other, in such a way that each allows the other to set out along its respective path."[2]

PRAYER

Let us entrust ourselves to the Virgin Mary, guardian of our faith.

Hail Mary, full of grace, the Lord is with thee. Blessed art thou among women and blessed is the fruit of thy womb, Jesus. Holy Mary,

---

1. "Mystical wisdom, which comes through love and is the object of these stanzas, need not be understood distinctly in order to cause love and affection in the soul, for it is given according to the mode of faith, through which we love God without understanding Him." John of the Cross, *Spiritual Canticle*, prol. par. 2.

2. Benedict XVI, Apostolic Letter *Porta Fidei* (Rome: Libreria Editrice Vaticana, October 11, 2011), par. 14.

Mother of God, pray for us, sinners, now and
at the hour of our death. Amen.

A Grace to Request

I ask the Lord that my faith may grow stronger,
that it may generate in my heart a great hope
and total trust in God, so that I may find—in
that faith and trust—the courage to love. I seek
to love all the people that the Lord puts in my
path with tender charity.

Light from a Faithful Witness

"Faith, hope and love are like three stars that
rise in the sky of our spiritual life to guide us to
God. They are the theological virtues *par excellence*: they put us in communion with God and
lead us to him. They form a triptych, whose apex
is found in love, the *agape* excellently praised by
Paul in a hymn of the First Letter to the Corinthians. It is sealed by the following declaration:
'So faith, hope, love abide, these three; but the
greatest of these is love' (1 Cor 13:13)."

—Pope St. John Paul II,
General Audience of November 22, 2000

Meditate on the Word

In the First Letter of Paul to the Corinthians, we find the following:

> If I speak in the tongues of mortals and of angels, but do not have love, I am a noisy gong or a clanging cymbal. And if I have prophetic powers, and understand all mysteries and all knowledge, and if I have all faith, so as to remove mountains, but do not have love, I am nothing. (1 Cor 13:1–2)

I keep in my heart and I repeat often this sentence:

"If I do not have love, I am nothing!"

Blessing

May the almighty and merciful God bless us and keep us. The Father, the Son, and the Holy Spirit. Amen.

Fifth Day

Faith Grows in Prayer

Daily Meditation

INVITATION TO CONTEMPLATION

I take a few moments to compose myself. I put myself in the present moment. . . . I breathe calmly. I put aside all worries and stress, and I confidently welcome God's presence. He is here, close to me, and he loves me.

SIGN OF THE CROSS

In the name of the Father, and of the Son, and of the Holy Spirit. Amen.

PRAYER TO THE HOLY SPIRIT

Holy Spirit, you who are light, you who are the consoler, come and guide my prayer today. Come fill me with your soft presence; awaken my heart to God's love. Make trust and faith grow in me.

MEDITATION FROM
FR. JACQUES PHILIPPE

The four preceding days, we have considered the importance of faith. It is faith that gives us life.

The question we are going to consider now for the next five days is, How do we grow in faith? How can faith be developed and strengthened in our lives?

The first response, and perhaps the most important one, is faithfulness to prayer. That is, persevering in prayer without getting discouraged, as Jesus says in the Gospel.

The first reason is that, as we've seen, faith is a gift from God, a grace that we thus should request from him without ceasing. In chapter nine of Mark's Gospel, there is this story of a father whose child is possessed by a demon who is torturing him, which the disciples can't expel. The father turns to Jesus, saying, "If you are able to do anything, have pity on us and help us!"

Jesus replies to them, "All things can be done for the one who believes." The father cries out then, "I believe; help my unbelief!"

This is a very beautiful prayer, which should be ours: "I believe, Lord, but help my unbelief!"

"Ask, and it will be given you; search, and you will find; knock, and the door will be opened for you" (Mt 7:7), Jesus says.

To grow in faith, the first thing to do is to ask for it, with perseverance, with insistence. God will give us what we request.

There's a second reason why prayer is so important for growing in faith, which is that faithfulness to prayer makes us exercise our faith.

The simplest and most normal way of expressing our faith, and therefore of making it grow, is to pray, addressing ourselves to God, putting ourselves in his presence.

The very fact of praying is an act of faith. If I pray, I believe that God exists, I believe that he is interested in me, and I believe that he loves me and listens to me.

Whatever form our prayer takes, whether it's request or thanksgiving, whether it simply keeps us in the divine presence or is a silent act of adoration of the Lord, prayer is always an act of faith.

Prayer puts us in contact with God and nourishes our faith. It makes us enter—sooner or later—into a living experience of God that will encourage our trust in him.

Faithful prayer establishes contact with God, and that is the most important thing. Even when it's about simply asking something of the Lord, the most important thing isn't the result of the prayer, which doesn't always conform to our expectations; rather, the very fact of addressing ourselves to God puts us in contact with him and thus changes something in us. Prayer isn't there to influence God, to change God, but to change something in us, through this contact with him.

In a mysterious but real way, contact with God through prayer nourishes our faith, encourages our hope, and increases our love.

This is true even if our prayer is poor! Praying isn't always about seeing, feeling, experiencing, or understanding. Even in the greatest poverty, in dry spells, even with distractions, if our prayer is an act of faith, it will really make us touch God, whose secret movements will little by little strengthen and grow our faith.

PRAYER

Let us entrust ourselves to the Virgin Mary, guardian of our faith.

> Hail Mary, full of grace, the Lord is with thee. Blessed art thou among women and blessed is the fruit of thy womb, Jesus. Holy Mary, Mother of God, pray for us, sinners, now and at the hour of our death. Amen.

A GRACE TO REQUEST

I ask for the grace of faithfulness to prayer. Even if it's sometimes poor or dry, it truly puts me in contact with him, and strengthens me in faith.

LIGHT FROM A FAITHFUL WITNESS

"It's faith that determines the quality of our relationship with God. Our whole prayer life is made up of this, of the conviction that our faith touches God."

—Bl. Marie-Eugène of the Child Jesus, OCD

MEDITATE ON THE WORD

In the Gospel of Luke, Jesus says the following:

> So, I say to you, Ask, and it will be given you;
> search, and you will find; knock, and the door
> will be opened for you. For everyone who asks
> receives, and everyone who searches finds,
> and for everyone who knocks, the door will
> be opened. Is there anyone among you who,
> if your child asks for a fish, will give a snake
> instead of a fish?
>
> Or if the child asks for an egg, will give a
> scorpion? If you then, who are evil, know how
> to give good gifts to your children, how much
> more will the heavenly Father give the Holy
> Spirit to those who ask him! (Lk 11:9–13)

BLESSING

May the almighty and merciful God bless us
and keep us. The Father, the Son, and the Holy
Spirit. Amen.

Sixth Day

FAITH PUT TO THE TEST

Daily Meditation

INVITATION TO CONTEMPLATION

I take a few moments to compose myself. I put myself in the present moment. . . . I breathe calmly. I put aside all worries and stress, and I confidently welcome God's presence. He is here, close to me, and he loves me.

SIGN OF THE CROSS

In the name of the Father, and of the Son, and of the Holy Spirit. Amen.

PRAYER TO THE HOLY SPIRIT

Holy Spirit, you who are light, you who are the consoler, come and guide my prayer today. Come fill me with your soft presence; awaken my heart to God's love. Make trust and faith grow in me.

MEDITATION FROM
FR. JACQUES PHILIPPE

As we've already seen, faith is often simple, easy, and joyful, but at other times it can become a struggle, a fight, or a decision that isn't spontaneous, but demands courage.

We all have lived through moments of difficulty and suffering, of deep darkness, which are a trial for our faith. What seemed evident before becomes problematic; we have doubts, questions without answers, or the occasionally sorrowful feeling that God is absent or has abandoned us. What is the Lord doing? Why has he left me to go through this? Can I really count on him? Why is he silent? All these questions and others assail us in a painful way.

The first thing that we should know is that this type of situation is normal in the spiritual life; all people go through trials in which it seems that God has contradicted himself and forgotten us.

I would even say that these times of trial are necessary. They make our illusions fall away, from our pride to our pretension of controlling everything. At these times, our faith is called to grow, to be more than a simple habit of thinking, but rather an adult decision that requires the engagement of our freedom.

Faith also becomes more pure. In effect, when we go through trials, faith can no longer rely solely on human things: an experience, a culture, habits, sentimental satisfaction, or benefits that we can measure. A certain emotional foundation to faith disappears, not so that faith diminishes, but on the contrary, so that it can be strengthened in relying more on God alone, on his word, on his promises.

God doesn't abandon us in these situations. In a hidden way, he sustains our faith and he fights in us.

After a terrible period of suffering and temptations, St. Catherine of Siena asked the Lord, "My Lord, where were you when my heart was disturbed by all those temptations?" Jesus responded to her, "I was in your heart . . . and I, who was defending your heart from the enemies, was hidden there all the time."

Thus being put to the test and going through the tempest, faith becomes stronger, in the end. In his first letter, the Apostle Peter has these beautiful words to say regarding this purification of faith through trial:

> In this you rejoice, even if now for a little while you have had to suffer various trials, so that the genuineness of your faith—being more precious than gold that, though perishable, is tested by fire—may be found to result in praise and glory and honor when Jesus Christ is revealed. (1 Pet 1:6–7)

What shall we do during these times of trial? We must not despair or be worried. We must persevere in prayer, confiding in God and making acts of faith and trust.

It's necessary to accept these difficult times, living one day at a time, humbly, simply, accepting that we cannot understand or master everything.

We must surrender ourselves into the hands of God in putting our hope in his faithfulness and his mercy. Of course, we must also sometimes share with someone who understands us and can help us.

One of the most precious things that God gives us during these times of trial are the words of Scripture. When we can no longer rely on our human capabilities and reasoning because everything seems vain and weak, we must rely on the words of Scripture, which have a grace, a particular authority that reaffirms our faith. Take, for example, when Jesus says to us: Do not fear, even all the hairs on your head are counted! (cf. Lk 12:7).

Every trial will end by the beginning of a new day of consolation and joy.

PRAYER

Let us entrust ourselves to the Virgin Mary, guardian of our faith.

> Hail Mary, full of grace, the Lord is with thee. Blessed art thou among women and blessed is the fruit of thy womb, Jesus. Holy Mary, Mother of God, pray for us, sinners, now and at the hour of our death. Amen.

A Grace to Request

I ask the Lord for the grace of never being discouraged during difficult times, of knowing how to abandon myself to him. I particularly confide in him the most painful and problematic thing that I'm going through today, telling him that I trust that he will be faithful.

Light from a Faithful Witness

"If you only knew what frightful thoughts obsess me! Pray very much for me in order that I do not listen to the devil who wants to persuade me about so many lies. It's the reasoning of the worst materialists which is imposed upon my mind. [. . .] O little Mother, must one have thoughts like this when one loves God so much! [. . .] I undergo them under duress, but while undergoing them I never cease making acts of faith."

—St. Thérèse of Lisieux

MEDITATE ON THE WORD

In the Book of Isaiah, we find the following:

> But Zion said, "The Lord has forsaken me, my Lord has forgotten me." Can a woman forget her nursing child, or show no compassion for the child of her womb? Even these may forget, yet I will not forget you. See, I have inscribed you on the palms of my hands. (Is 49:14–16)

I memorize and repeat this phrase often:

"I will never forget you, for I've inscribed you on the palms of my hands."

BLESSING

May the almighty and merciful God bless us and keep us. The Father, the Son, and the Holy Spirit. Amen.

Seventh Day

LIVING IN THE SIMPLICITY OF FAITH

Daily Meditation

INVITATION TO CONTEMPLATION

I take a few moments to compose myself. I put myself in the present moment. . . . I breathe calmly. I put aside all worries and stress, and I confidently welcome God's presence. He is here, close to me, and he loves me.

SIGN OF THE CROSS

In the name of the Father, and of the Son, and of the Holy Spirit. Amen

PRAYER TO THE HOLY SPIRIT

Holy Spirit, you who are light, you who are the consoler, come and guide my prayer today. Come fill me with your soft presence; awaken my heart to God's love. Make trust and faith grow in me.

MEDITATION FROM
FR. JACQUES PHILIPPE

We again ask ourselves the question, How do we grow in faith?

One of the requirements for this growth is to be vigilant in keeping—through all circumstances—what I'll call a "spirit of faith," and avoiding whatever could be contrary to this spirit of faith. It's about remaining in the simplicity of our Christian faith, in a way.

Let's look at some examples.

We often have questions, doubts, and temptations when it comes to faith. This is normal. But we must not ruminate on them and dwell on them. Of course, it's good to reflect on these things and look for answers, to inform ourselves, but sometimes we should just accept that we won't understand everything and can't explain everything, welcoming with trust and humility the faith of the Church.

Nor should we always be looking for extraordinary and new things that are more likely to satisfy our curiosity than to make us really grow in love and charity. We must not always want to feel and taste things, but rather to accept the arid moments of the dry spells we go through.

It's sort of the same with the sequence of events of our lives. We must try to understand, to reflect, and to find solutions and appropriate responses. But sometimes, we must know how to set aside certain concerns, not going around and around indefinitely on the "whys" that don't always have an answer. It means trusting ourselves entirely to God by accepting that we may not understand and master everything in our life.

We pretend to be able to explain everything; we have this need to find answers to everything, which is more the result of the human need for reassurance, rather than a real quest for truth.

One of the particular faults of our day is the desire to be informed about everything, always being up-to-date on the latest novelty, which nourishes an insatiable curiosity that makes us lose the simplicity of our faith. What saves us isn't an abundance of knowledge and information, but faith and abandonment to God's hands. Gustave Thibon said, "When I need something new, I read St. Paul!" The latest news gets stale very quickly, and the only real novelty is the love of God. This love is always new and young!

Another frequent attitude that's contrary to the spirit of faith is the worrisome search for human security: always wanting to be secure financially, emotionally, intellectually, or otherwise; always wanting to have enough strength, education, competence, and means to do one thing or another, all in the fear of being caught off guard. We have to accept the security that is given to us, doing our best to acquire and get ahead with prudence. An excessive need for security and assurance ends up completely killing the spirit of faith, and stops us from experiencing God's faithfulness and power, which is displayed through the weakness of mankind.

One last remark: We can't just consider human circumstances, whether they be the good or bad actions and decisions of others or the different responsibilities or causes that can intervene in a situation. Living in a spirit of faith means believing that in the end everything is in the hands of God. There are, of course, things that God didn't want, which are the result of human errors, but God permits them and we must accept them, rather than remaining bitter and angry. We should be convinced that we are in the hands of God and are not victims of circumstances or the errors of others.

St. Thérèse of Lisieux expresses it this way: "I am a weak reed that cannot break since, whatever happens to it, it only wants to see the sweet hand of Jesus." This simplicity of faith is a source of great peace and freedom in the end.

PRAYER

Let us entrust ourselves to the Virgin Mary, guardian of our faith.

> Hail Mary, full of grace, the Lord is with thee. Blessed art thou among women and blessed is the fruit of thy womb, Jesus. Holy Mary, Mother of God, pray for us, sinners, now and at the hour of our death. Amen.

A Grace to Request

I ask God for the grace to live more in a spirit of faith. Accepting what is beyond me, and not only considering human circumstance and explanations, but seeing in all things the hand of God who can bring good out of anything.

Light from a Faithful Witness

"You cling too fast to these doubts and fears. You concentrate upon them too much instead of ignoring them and casting yourself upon God in utter self-abandonment.

"Only through this happy and holy self-abandonment, can you ever enjoy an enduring peace."

—Letter of Fr. Jean-Pierre de Caussade, SJ, to a religious sister who confided her distress to him[1]

"God's Providence is so all-encompassing that nothing falls outside of it and that even sin finds its proper place in it, so also, our surrender

1. Fr. Jean-Pierre de Caussade, SJ, *Self-Abandonment to Divine Providence* (Gastonia, NC: TAN Books, 2013).

ought to be so perfect that even our worry, our
troubles, and our temptations are enclosed in it
and fall into place in it. Not even our troubles
need to be a source of trouble. We cannot always
live in total peace."

—Fr. Wilfrid Stinissen, OCD,
Into Your Hands, Father[2]

Meditate on the Word

In the Gospel of Saint Luke, we find the following words from Jesus:

> Are not five sparrows sold for two pennies?
> Yet not one of them is forgotten in God's
> sight. But even the hairs of your head are all
> counted. Do not be afraid; you are of more
> value than many sparrows. (Lk 12:6–7)

I memorize this sentence and repeat it often:

"The hairs of your head are all counted. Do
not be afraid."

---

2. Fr. Wilfrid Stinissen, OCD, *Into Your Hands, Father: Aban-
doning Ourselves to the God Who Loves Us* (San Francisco: Igna-
tius Press, 2011), p. 32.

BLESSING

May the almighty and merciful God bless us
and keep us. The Father, the Son, and the Holy
Spirit. Amen.

Eighth Day

Celebrating, Sharing, and Declaring Our Faith

Daily Meditation

INVITATION TO CONTEMPLATION

I take a few moments to compose myself. I put myself in the present moment. . . . I breathe calmly. I put aside all worries and stress, and I confidently welcome God's presence. He is here, close to me, and he loves me.

SIGN OF THE CROSS

In the name of the Father, and of the Son, and of the Holy Spirit. Amen.

PRAYER TO THE HOLY SPIRIT

Holy Spirit, you who are light, you who are the consoler, come and guide my prayer today. Come fill me with your soft presence; awaken my heart to God's love. Make trust and faith grow in me.

MEDITATION FROM
FR. JACQUES PHILIPPE

How do we grow in faith? One of the best ways is to share it with others.

Faith, as we've said, is a very personal, intimate decision, but it also has a strong community dimension. My faith is the faith of the Church. Faith makes all the believers adhere to a single reality, thus putting us in communion with each other.

In the Letter to the Ephesians, St. Paul puts it this way: "There is one body and one Spirit, just as you were called to the one hope of your calling, one Lord, one faith, one baptism, one God and Father of all, who is above all and through all and in all" (Eph 4:4–6).

We can't be a Christian all alone, in an individualistic way. Faith is received, and it must also be transmitted.

An essential way of growing in the faith is to celebrate it and share it with others. Proclaiming the faith—even singing it—with others strengthens it and makes it grow.

The liturgical assembly and the different forms of communal prayer are very beautiful ways of celebrating, proclaiming, and singing the faith together. Faith should not be merely kept in the heart. It should be externalized: spoken, sung, and even sometimes danced in order to become more alive.

We must both witness to others about our faith and listen to the testimonies of faith from our brothers and sisters in Christ for mutual encouragement.

At the beginning of the Letter to the Romans, St. Paul expresses it this way: "I am longing to see you so that I may share with you some spiritual gift to strengthen you—or rather so that we may be mutually encouraged by each other's faith, both yours and mine" (Rom 1:11–12).

Paul knows that in visiting this community in Rome, as yet unfamiliar to him, he not only will encourage them in their faith, but also will be strengthened in his own faith by meeting them.

I remember a moment at the beginning of my community life in Jerusalem, one day when I was a little sad and depressed. The person in charge of the community asked me to welcome a young couple who was visiting us and who was interested in the Christian faith, wanting me to speak to them about my conversion and my entrance into the community. I went with lead feet, but little by little as I spoke, I remembered all of God's interventions in my life, and I quickly regained the joy and high spirits that had left me! I don't know if my testimony did them any good, but it did a whole lot of good for me, in any case!

Our faith also grows each time we have the courage to declare it to others. Faith is one of those good things that increases when we share it.

There's a surprising thing in the last chapter of Mark's Gospel. Jesus, before ascending into heaven, reproaches the disciples for their slowness to believe and for their doubts, and yet he sends them immediately to preach the Gospel all over the world.

He knows very well that in announcing the Good News to others, in aiding the Holy Spirit's work in the hearts of people by going to speak to them, the disciples' own faith will grow and be affirmed.

It's the same for us today. If we conserve our faith, limiting it to just a little corner of our lives as a purely private affair, if we never have the audacity to witness to it and to declare it, there's a strong risk that it will wither.

Our witnessing should be humble and respectful toward others, of course, but if we want our faith to be living and strong, we shouldn't pass up opportunities we are given to speak of it and to witness to it. This does not mean that we will succeed in convincing everyone; we must stay very humble, knowing that only God can open hearts. However, whether it is received or not, our testimony of faith will always make us grow.

PRAYER

Let us entrust ourselves to the Virgin Mary, guardian of our faith.

Hail Mary, full of grace, the Lord is with thee. Blessed art thou among women and blessed is the fruit of thy womb, Jesus. Holy Mary,

Mother of God, pray for us, sinners, now and at the hour of our death. Amen.

A Grace to Request

Faith is a good thing that grows in being shared. I ask for the grace to find more joy in celebrating and singing my faith with others. I also ask for the grace not to miss opportunities to witness to others about it when the Holy Spirit invites me to do so.

Light from a Faithful Witness

"St. Paul kept the faith because, in the same way that he received it, he gave it away, he went out to the fringes, and didn't dig himself into defensive positions."

—Pope Francis, Homily from
October 27, 2013

Meditate on the Word

In the Gospel of Saint Matthew, we find the following:

Again, truly I tell you, if two of you agree on earth about anything you ask, it will be done for you by my Father in heaven. For where two or three are gathered in my name, I am there among them. (Mt 18:19–20)

I memorize and repeat this phrase often:

"Where two or three are gathered in my name, I am there among them."

BLESSING

May the almighty and merciful God bless us and keep us. The Father, the Son, and the Holy Spirit. Amen.

Ninth Day

GIVING OURSELVES
TO MARY TO PARTAKE
IN HER FAITH

Daily Meditation

INVITATION TO CONTEMPLATION

I take a few moments to compose myself. I put myself in the present moment. . . . I breathe calmly. I put aside all worries and stress, and I confidently welcome God's presence. He is here, close to me, and he loves me.

SIGN OF THE CROSS

In the name of the Father, and of the Son, and of the Holy Spirit. Amen.

PRAYER TO THE HOLY SPIRIT

Holy Spirit, you who are light, you who are the consoler, come and guide my prayer today. Come fill me with your soft presence; awaken my heart to God's love. Make trust and faith grow in me.

MEDITATION FROM
FR. JACQUES PHILIPPE

The last way of growing in faith upon which we'll meditate is entrusting ourselves to the Virgin Mary. It's not a question of a more or less optional devotion, but something much more profound.

As the Second Vatican Council reminds us, what makes Mary so great is, above all, the greatness of her faith, a faith even greater than Abraham's.

All of Mary's life was a pilgrimage in faith, as the Gospels show.

Mary also, as Pope St. John Paul II has said, is the creature who lived through the most arduous trial of all, the darkest night of faith that anyone has ever known.

At the foot of the Cross, Mary sees her son rejected by all, seemingly abandoned by God, subject to an atrocious and unjust torture.

In this moment when all of God's promises seemed completely contradicted, Mary remained faithful, upright in faith, hoping against all hope, offering in the suffering the consent of her love. She kept the words she heard from the angel Gabriel at the moment of the Annunciation in her heart: "Nothing will be impossible with God" (cf. Lk 1:37). She continued to believe that all of God's promises would be accomplished.

For this reason, Mary received the grace to be the mother and guardian of the faith of the Church. She keeps the faith and hope of believers alive, even through the worst trials.

In his book *A Treatise on True Devotion to the Blessed Virgin*, St. Louis-Marie de Montfort exposes a very beautiful truth: If we accept Mary as our mother, as Jesus invites us to do just before dying ("Then he said to the disciple, 'Here is your mother'" cf. Jn 19:27), if we give ourselves entirely to Mary, then Mary will give herself entirely to us, and we will take part in the graces that she has received from God. "She also gives her whole self, and gives it in an unspeakable manner, to him who gives all to her."

The principal thing that Mary wants to give to her children is her faith, because it's the most precious gift that she has received from God, and the most necessary gift for the Church.

It's the biggest present that she desires to share with us.

To conclude, let us listen to the splendid way that St. Louis-Marie de Montfort describes this faith that Mary wants to transmit:

Our Blessed Lady will give you also a portion of her faith, which was the greatest of all faiths that ever were on earth, greater than the faith of all the Patriarchs, Prophets, Apostles, and Saints put together. [. . .] A pure faith which will make you hardly care at all about the sensible and the extraordinary; a lively faith animated by charity, which will enable you to perform all your actions from the motive of pure love; a faith firm and immovable as a rock, through which you will rest quiet and constant in the midst of storms and hurricanes; a faith active and piercing, which, like a mysterious pass-key, will give you entrance into all the mysteries of Jesus, into the Last Ends of man, and into the Heart of God Himself; a courageous faith, which will enable you to undertake and carry out without hesitation great things for God and for the salvation of souls; lastly, a faith which will be your blazing torch, your divine life, your hidden treasure of divine wisdom, and your omnipotent arm, which you will use to enlighten those who are in the darkness of the shadow of death, to inflame those who are lukewarm and who have need of the heated gold of charity, to give life to those who are dead in sin, to teach and overthrow, by your meek and powerful words, the hearts of marble and the cedars of Lebanon, and finally, to resist the devil and all the enemies of salvation.*

Prayer

Let us entrust ourselves to the Virgin Mary, guardian of our faith.

> Hail Mary, full of grace, the Lord is with thee. Blessed art thou among women and blessed

---

* Translator's note: Philippe cites as: *Traité de la vraie dévotion à la Sainte Vierge*, Médiaspaul, p. 223. You can also find at: *https://www.ecatholic2000.com/montfort/true/devotion.shtml# __RefHeading___Toc332751807*

is the fruit of thy womb, Jesus. Holy Mary, Mother of God, pray for us, sinners, now and at the hour of our death. Amen.

A Grace to Request

Let us ask for the grace to welcome Mary as our mother, to "take her into our own home" as the Apostle John did (cf. Jn 19:27). Let us ask for the grace to give ourselves entirely to her with full trust, to live in her sweet presence all the days of our lives. Let us ask Mary to spread to us her pure, strong faith.

Light from a Faithful Witness

"The more we open ourselves to God, welcome the gift of faith and put our whole trust in him—like Abraham, like Mary—the more capable he will make us, with his presence, of living every situation of life in peace and assured of his faithfulness and his love."

—Pope Emeritus Benedict XVI,
General Audience of December 19, 2012

Meditate on the Word

In the Gospel of Luke, we find the following:

> Elizabeth was filled with the Holy Spirit and exclaimed with a loud cry, "Blessed are you among women, and blessed is the fruit of your womb. And why has this happened to me, that the mother of my Lord comes to me? For as soon as I heard the sound of your greeting, the child in my womb leaped for joy. And blessed is she who believed that there would be a fulfillment of what was spoken to her by the Lord." (Lk 1:41–45)

I memorize and repeat this sentence regularly:

"Blessed is she who believed that there would be a fulfilment of what was spoken to her by the Lord."

Blessing

May the almighty and merciful God bless us and keep us. The Father, the Son, and the Holy Spirit. Amen.

Photo Credits

Day 1: *The Nativity*, Gari Melchers (American, 1860–1932), c. 1891, Gari Melchers Home and Studio, University of Mary Washington.

Day 2: *Christ Gives the Keys of Heaven to Saint Peter*, Peter Paul Rubens (1577–1640), oil on panel, c. 1613/15.

Day 3: *Baptism of Christ*, Bartolomeo Coda, exhibited at the Great Masters of the Renaissance in Zagreb, Croatia, December 12, 2011.

Day 4: *The Incredulity of St. Thomas*, Michelangelo Merisi Da Caravaggio (1571–1610), oil on canvas, 1601/2.

Day 5: *The Angelus*, Jean Francois Millet (1817–1875), c. 1857–9, Musee d'Orsay, Paris.

Day 6: Detail of *Flagellation*, Michelangelo Merisi Da Caravaggio (1571–1610), Baroque, 1607–1608, National Museum of Capodimonte, Naples, Italy.

Day 7: Detail of *The Holy Family*, Adolfo Magrini (1874–1947), 1895, Italy.

Day 8: *The Visitation of Mary*, Upper Rheinish Master, from shutters of an altarpiece of John the Baptist history, 1400–1435, Upper Rhine Valley, Staatliche Kunsthalle Karlsruhe Museum, Germany.

Day 9: *Virgin Mary*, Peruvian Religious Art, Alamy Stock Photo.